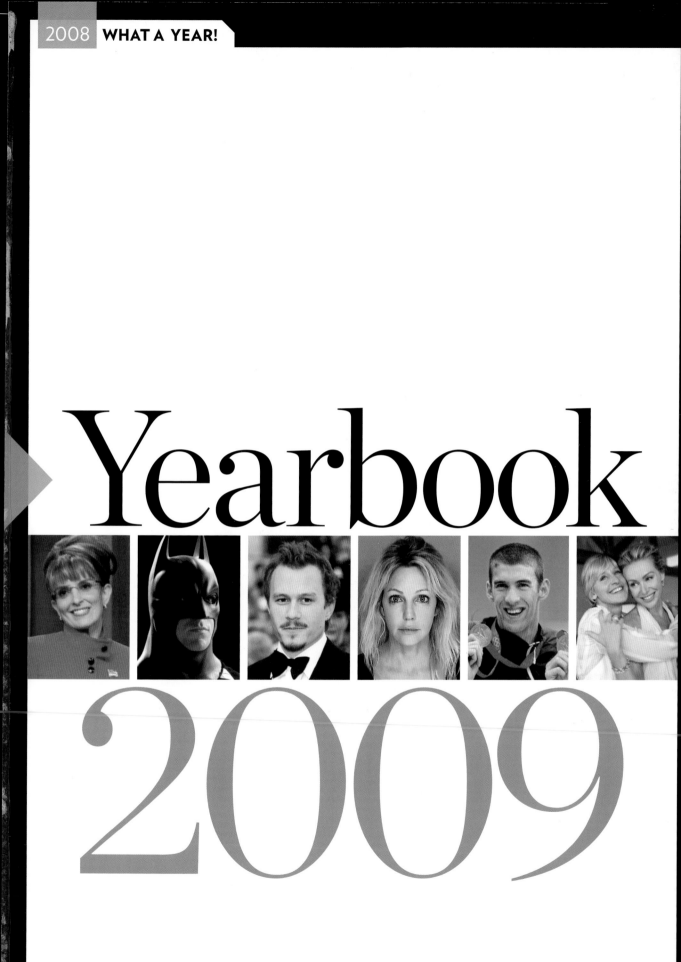

Yearbook

2009

History and Hope

Yes, he did! By reaching a new generation of voters and riding a sweeping tide of change, Barack Obama became the first African-American to win the White House

FIRST FAMILY
The Obamas (with Sasha, left, and Malia) "have been so honorable throughout the whole campaign," Michelle's mother, Marian, told PEOPLE.

NO MATTER WHAT HAPPENS IN THE NEXT FOUR years, Tuesday night, Nov. 4, 2008, will always be a "Where were you when . . . ?" moment. Crowds chanting "Yes, we can!" gathered outside the White House. In Harlem celebrants danced and wept. In Chicago's Grant Park more than 200,000 people hugged and shrieked as TV networks flashed the news: Barack Hussein Obama had just been elected the 44th President of the United States. A few miles away, in a suite at the Hyatt Regency Chicago, the mood was more subdued: Obama, 47, sat on a sofa beside his mother-in-law, Marian Robinson, monitoring the election returns. When CNN made the

MAMA OBAMA
Obama (during the campaign, above, and with his Kansas-born mother, Ann, in the '60s) has called her "the dominant figure in my formative years."

official call shortly before 10 p.m., "Everybody was quiet," Robinson, 71, recalled. "We weren't like the people in the stands—you know, yelling and screaming."

Though Obama had made a point of *not* making a point of his skin color throughout his 21-month campaign, it was impossible on that night to ignore the astonishingly obvious: Americans had just elected their first African-American President. As Obama stepped out in Grant Park to greet his supporters—their tears, his joy separated by plates of 8-ft.-high bullet-proof glass—Obama deftly acknowledged the historic moment without mentioning the word race. "If there is anyone out there who still doubts that America

can role models to fill the void left by a father he met only once after his parents split up when he was just a toddler. Along an educational trajectory that ended at Harvard Law School, he laid claim to the "Barack" of his African heritage and discovered his talent as a consensus builder. "He just had a profile far broader than the diversity issues," recalled fellow student Artur Davis, now a U.S. congressman from Alabama. That talent for finding common ground, coupled with a dazzling gift for oratory, not only left more seasoned challengers echoing his message of "change" but ignited a grassroots revolution that on election night made a purple mush of the red-state/blue-state jigsaw puzzle.

ABSENT DAD Obama's Kenyan father, Barack Sr., only saw his son once after the couple divorced in '64.

GRANDPARENTS Obama lost Madelyn (with him and husband Stanley) just two days before the election.

is a place where all things are possible," he opened his victory speech, "who still wonders if the dream of our founders is alive in our time, who still questions the power of our democracy, tonight is your answer."

It is not the answer many would have predicted with confidence back in February 2007, when Obama entered a crowded Democratic field with only two-thirds of his first term as Illinois' junior senator under his belt. A self-described "skinny kid with the funny name," Obama, by his own admission, spent the first half of his life trying to figure out who he was: black, like his Kenyan father, or white, like his mom from Kansas? Growing up in Hawaii and Indonesia, he went by the name Barry and vainly searched for African-Ameri-

After his election, Obama retired to his six-bedroom home in Chicago's South Side. While an ailing economy, two wars and energy issues all commanded his attention, he and his wife of 16 years, Michelle, 44, made clear that job No. 1 was holding life steady for their two daughters, Malia, 10, and Sasha, 7. "If I ever thought this was ruining my family," Obama told PEOPLE three months before his election, "I wouldn't do it." As Americans wallowed in Obama-thrall—What musicians will Michelle invite to the White House? What kind of dog will the girls get?—the President-elect got down to work. "We are facing the greatest economic challenge of our lifetime," he said in a radio address four days after his election. "We don't have a moment to lose."

" America is
a place where
all things are
possible . . . the
dream of our
founders is alive
"

CROWD PLEASER
Obama drew tens of thousands to a speech in St. Louis in October. Inset, the Obamas in Chicago right after his historic victory.

SHE CAME OUT OF NOWHERE—AND WAS-illa, Alaska, pop. 7,028—to become the second biggest political star of the year. No scriptwriter could have conjured her without getting canned: the hunky hubby who's a snowmobile champ; the pregnant, unwed teen daughter; the folksy, fumbling interviews ("you betcha!"); and that famous field-dressed moose.

Yet give Caribou Barbie her due: As John McCain's running mate, the Alaska governor jazzed up a flagging campaign, guested on *Saturday Night Live* (alongside arch-imitator Tina Fey) and inspired a million Halloween costumes. So now what? "I can always go home again and just be Mom," she told PEOPLE. Or might she rear that bouffant again in, say, about four years?

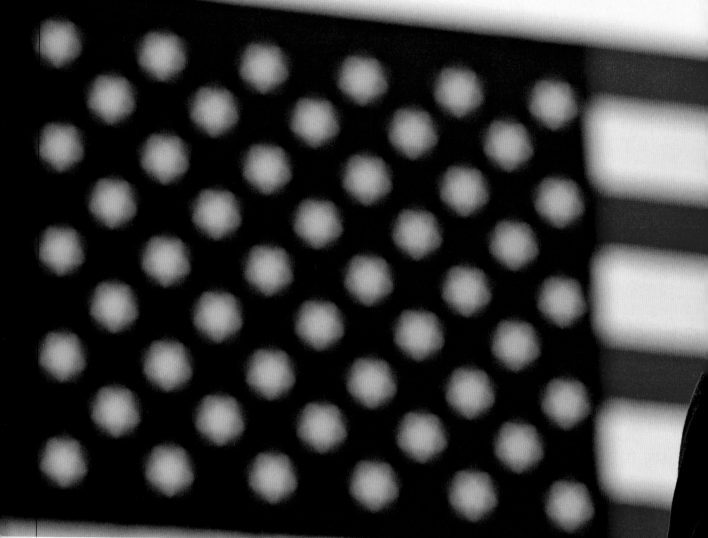

SARAH SNAPBOOK
Palin (from left) in high school in '82; as Miss Wasilla in '84; after a caribou kill; in Kuwait in '07; with husband Todd and kids Trig, Piper, Bristol and Willow in June; with runnning mate McCain; campaigning in Colorado in October.

Sarah Palin

Heath Ledger

(1979–2008)

FALLEN STAR
"He was trying to lead a healthy life," a friend said of Ledger (in 2005). "But sometimes he went to excess."

"

[Family] is
everything to me—
before, I felt like I
was floating through
life, like a ghost

"

HE HAD JUST WRAPPED THE ROLE OF his life—as a jarringly clownish Joker in *The Dark Knight*—and was, it seemed, on the cusp of full-blown stardom. But Heath Ledger, the rugged young Aussie actor with a tender and wistful grace, would not live to see it: Early on Jan. 22 police found him in his $23,000-a-month Manhattan loft, dead from an accidental drug overdose. Friends said Ledger, 28, was known for his partying and drug use; at the time of his death he was also exhausted from the long *Batman* shoot, worn down by pneumonia and insomnia and depressed over his split from his *Brokeback Mountain* costar Michelle Williams, 28, the mother of their 3-year-old daughter Matilda Rose, whom he didn't get to see over the Christmas holidays. "He said, 'I'm missing my girl,'" recalled a friend who spoke with him a day before his death. Weak and vulnerable, he overdosed on a cocktail of prescription sleep aids and antianxiety pills.

His death hit Hollywood hard—and devastated Williams. "It's one thing to lose someone close to you," said a friend. "But the fact that she lost Matilda's father is crushing." There were rumors about Ledger's last days (his massage therapist, who found the body, had phoned his friend Mary-Kate Olsen before calling police) and reports of a rift over Ledger's will, which was written before he met Williams and left his $20 million estate to his family in Australia (his father, Kim, later explained, "Our family has gifted everything to Matilda."). Critics praised Ledger's pasty-faced Joker and predicted a posthumous Oscar; Williams, meanwhile, tried to move on, dating director Spike Jonze and working hard to make her daughter's days seem as normal as possible. Yet she kept living in the couple's beloved Brooklyn townhouse and vowed that Matilda, the spitting image of Ledger, would not soon forget her dad. She "will be brought up with the best memories of him," Williams said. That, too, is how the world will remember Ledger: a gifted actor and delicate soul, gone far too soon.

DOTING DAD "He cared so much for his baby," a friend says of Ledger (with Matilda in 2007).

FAIRY TALE
"They were kindred spirits," a friend says of Williams and Ledger (at the Oscars in 2006).

THE DARK KNIGHT 2008

BROKEBACK MOUNTAIN 2005

THE PATRIOT 2000

Britney's Wild Ride

The singer seemed to finally hit bottom before taking control of her life again

ON THE UPSWING Spears with Jayden and Sean Preston and a friend Oct. 23; at the MTV Awards Sept. 7; with Neil Patrick Harris on *How I Met Your Mother* May 12.

HER 2007 WAS BAD ENOUGH— shaving her head; bombing on MTV; losing custody of sons Preston, 3, and Jayden, 2. Then 2008 kicked off even worse. On Jan. 3 paramedics strapped a wild-eyed Spears to a gurney and whisked her to a psych ward after she had locked herself and Jayden in the bathroom of her L.A. home and forced a four-hour stand-off with police. Said a source close to the 27-year-old pop star: "She came totally unglued." Yet with the meltdown, she turned a corner. Her father, Jamie, took charge of her life (a judge named him legal conservator), while Spears dealt with her problems and, after just under a week in a hospital, steered clear of the spotlight. Back in the recording studio she cut a new single, *Piece of Me,* and won three MTV awards in October. On the show a healthy-looking Spears thanked "my two beautiful boys for just inspiring me every day."

SURVIVAL
Thousands of children died when poorly built schools collapsed. The quake, which registered 7.9, and its aftershocks destroyed more than 400,000 buildings.

THE MAY 12 EARTHQUAKE JOLTED not only Sichuan province but also, in the days that followed, all of China. More than 70,000 people died, many of them children trapped in shoddily built schools. Refusing to be silenced by authorities, outraged parents demanded local officials and contractors be investigated. "Otherwise," said one distraught father, "there are a thousand parents who would beat them to death." But there were also surprising, positive notes in the aftermath: China's government, so often slow and secretive, acted swiftly and publicly to provide relief. And China's citizens, often reluctant to get involved, surprised themselves by volunteering by the thousands and raising money as never before. "We Chinese people are growing closer and closer together," said one volunteer. "And because of that, the country's morality is rising too."

The Big Quake

Beijing Bling

LUCKY CHARM
At the rate Phelps was kissing gold medals, it's a wonder he didn't get chapped lips.

My goal is to change the sport of swimming

HE WAS BOTH INVIN-cible and humble. "I'm not unbeatable," he said. "No one is unbeatable." Except for Michael Phelps, for two history-making weeks in August. The 6'4" Marylander not only won eight gold medals—the most by any athlete in any Olympics—but did it with enough drama to make any screenwriter proud. Phelps, 23, did it with ease, and he did it with help: Teammate's Jason Lezak's heroic anchor leg in the 4 x 100 free-style relay gave the U.S. the win by .08 seconds. He did it when rivals trash-talked ("Go ahead," urged a USA Swimming official, "poke the tiger with the stick"), and he did it even when others feared he hadn't (many thought Phelps had been out-touched in the 100 butterfly; technology and underwater cameras told a different story). Proud and exhausted after 17 races in eight events, he finished with a huge grin and a plan: "I'm going to sit on the beach and do nothing," he said. "I'm sleeping in."

GOLD FEAT
In the 100, the gap between Bolt and the competition was startling.

Lightning Strikes Thrice

I T WAS HARD, PROBABLY, EVEN FOR THE CAMERAS to believe: Competing in the Olympics 100-meter dash—and, unofficially, for the title of world's fastest man—Jamaican sprinter Usain "Lightning" Bolt was so far ahead that, 15 meters before the finish, *he began to decelerate and start his celebration*—and *still* set a world record. Four days later—after promising, "Tonight I'm going to race the whole thing"—he broke Michael Johnson's 12-year-old record in the 200, a mark many had thought would last for decades. Not surprisingly, the exuberant 6'5" Bolt also helped Jamaica's men win the 4 x 100 relay, again in world-record time. Something to think about: At 22, "he's really new at this," said a fellow runner. "He's not like anything we've ever seen—and he's still learning."

She was the Energizer Bunny of the U.S. women's gymnastics team—spinning, jumping, tumbling and, somehow, always smiling. Shawn Johnson, 4'9" and 16 years old, radiated giddy enthusiasm just walking to and from the gymnastics venue. The Des Moines, Iowa, high school junior helped the U.S. women win silver (the Chinese took gold) in the team competition; took silver again (just behind friend and Olympics roommate Nastia Liukin) in the individual All-Around competition; won a third silver in floor exercise and—in her final Beijing Olympics appearance—won gold in the balance beam.

GOLD METTLE
Johnson smiled through a grueling week—and took home three silvers and a gold.

Small Wonder

Cult Clash

ALLEGING THAT A POLYGAMIST SECT had sanctioned physical and sexual abuse— including marriages of underage girls— authorities raided the Yearning for Zion Ranch in Eldorado, Texas, in April and took 460 children into protective custody. The action sparked complex debates about religious, parental and children's rights. Eventually, even though the cult's leader Warren Jeffs had been convicted in 2007 of aiding in the rape of a 14-year-old girl, Texas courts concluded that the authorities had acted without sufficient evidence of wrongdoing and ordered the children returned. Simultaneously, the sect's leaders said they would officially renounce underage marriage.

ROUNDED UP
Sect members (right) wept after the raid. Above: On April 6, mothers and children were bused to a facility. "We are not abused," insisted one mom. "You can put an exclamation by it!"

GO AHEAD, GET 'EM OUT OF YOUR SYSTEM. He's got the blues. He's blue in the face. So how'd the Blue Man Group audition go? In fact, landscaper Paul Karason, 57, has a condition called argyria, the result of his fascination with an alternative and controversial medical treatment involving colloidal silver. Using a generator that turns distilled water and silver wire into the chalky liquid remedy, he drank a tumbler of it every day for several years, believing it cured his acid reflux, sinus trouble and arthritis. When he developed a case of dermatitis, he started rubbing the silver right onto his face—and, within a year, turned blue. "It was so gradual I didn't notice," he says. Divorced and living with a girlfriend—to whom beauty, apparently, isn't just skin deep—he now drinks only small doses of the colloidal silver, and handles gasps and stares with humor. "Sometimes," he explains, "I'll tell people I'm from another planet."

AM I BLUE? YOU BET
"In a way," says Karason, "I take pleasure in being unique."

Yep, I'm Blue

He Had a Baby!

EGALLY, HE'S THOMAS Beatie, an Oregon T-shirt business owner and husband. But the world knows him as the Pregnant Man, a former Girl Scout and female model who took testosterone and transitioned to a male—yet kept his female reproductive organs and, in June, gave birth to a healthy 9-lb. 5-oz. daughter, Susan Juliette. "I am always going to be Susan's father," says Beatie, 34, who considers his wife, Nancy, 46, the mother. "Giving birth didn't change that at all."

MANTERNITY
"We know prejudice is out there," says Beatie (with Nancy in March, left, and with their daughter in July). "But how can anyone judge this beautiful little baby?"

The Screamer

ENMESHED IN A BITTER DIVorce, Tricia Walsh-Smith, 52, became an Internet sensation (3 million hits) when she posted an invective-filled rant against her husband, Philip Smith, 77, on YouTube. The strategy may have backfired: Three months later Philip was granted a divorce on grounds of "cruel and inhuman treatment"—with no change in the couple's 1999 prenup.

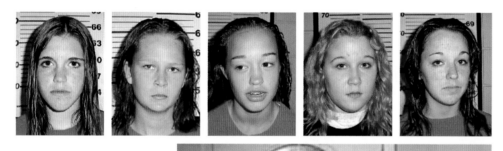

Mean Girls

IT WAS, QUITE SIMPLY, the girl fight seen round the world. In a three-minute tape that made its way onto YouTube, a gang of Florida girls is seen pummeling erstwhile pal Tori Lindsay, 16, in a living room as she pleads to leave. A complaint from Lindsay led to the arrest of six girls and two boys who allegedly served as lookouts; all were slapped with adult charges of battery and kidnapping. (Charges were subsequently dropped against one girl and the two boys.) "Our great sheriff made a mountain out of a molehill," said the father of one of the accused.

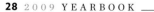

MySpace Justice

THE STORY WAS sad, then it became shocking: In October 2006, Megan Meier, 13, an emotionally fragile teen who had been taking antidepressants, hanged herself after "Josh," a boy she had recently been flirting with on MySpace, abruptly turned on her and told her "the world would be better off" without her. Then came the breathtaking revelation: "Josh" was a fiction, created by one of Megan's Dardenne Prairie, Mo., neighbors, Lori Drew, 49, to torment the teenager. In November, Drew was convicted on three misdemeanor counts that carry up to three years in prison and a $300,000 fine when she is sentenced early in 2009.

TRAGEDY Tina Meier, with pictures of her late daughter Megan; tormentor Lori Drew (above) was found guilty.

HEARTBREAKING MYSTERY
DNA samples from the crime scene match those in other Reno attacks.

Taken in the Night

IT WAS THE SORT OF crime at the heart of anyone's nightmare: On Jan. 19 Brianna Denison, 19, a student at Santa Barbara City College, attended some parties in Reno, then crashed on a friend's couch. When her friend looked in the next morning, Denison was missing, the glass-panel front door—which offered a view of the couch—was unlocked, and there was a bloodstain on a pillow. One month later her body was found in a field; DNA evidence links her killer to two earlier sexual attacks against local college women. The killer is still at large.

Bel Air Studio ©2005

Murder
in the
Marines

ACCUSED
While on the run, Laurean claimed Lauterbach had killed herself and that he had only buried her.

BY LATE IN THE YEAR, LITTLE in the case was certain—except that the remains of Lance Cpl. Maria Lauterbach, 20, eight months pregnant, had been found buried in the yard of another Camp Lejeune, N.C., Marine: Cpl. Cesar Laurean, 21, whom she had accused of rape. Laurean fled after the body was found in January and was arrested in Mexico three months later. Charged with first-degree murder, Laurean faces extradition.

Bon Mariage!

CALL IT DEJA VU WITH A DIF-ference: In late 2007, French President Nicolas Sarkozy, 53 and freshly divorced, took his new romance public by strolling Versailles' gardens with Italian ex-model Carla Bruni, 39. Two months later, they took another walk in the same park—but this time both wore wedding rings. Earlier, the pair had exchanged vows in a brief civil ceremony. "I'm very glad for my daughter," said her mother. "And also certainly for the president."

FIRST LADY
Bruni, who once dated Mick Jagger, will now spend her nights together with the President of France.

SHE IS TALL AND GRACEFUL, AND THERE isn't anything guarded about her. But six years ago Elizabeth Smart's life changed forever when a drifter named Brian David Mitchell allegedly kidnapped her from her parents' Salt Lake City home and held her captive for nine months. Rescued in March '03, Smart has rarely spoken about her ordeal. But she agreed to talk with PEOPLE because she wanted her story to help other children who have survived abductions. "I feel so fortunate that I was able to come through this unscarred," she said. "I want to tell other people, 'Don't give up. Miracles do happen.'" Family and friends report Smart, 21, is doing remarkably well. Now living 40 miles from home at Brigham Young University, she majors in music performance, though a concert career playing the harp may not be in her future. "There are so many other things I want to do," she said, including helping her father pursue child-protection legislation. "I only have one life, and I'm not going to miss out on it," she said. "When I'm through, I want to be able to say, 'Wow, I lived a great life.'"

ELIZABETH'S ORDEAL
Taken at knifepoint, Smart was chained to a tree during her captivity. The two people charged with her kidnapping are being held at a Utah psychiatric hospital.

Elizabeth Smart

AS A WHITE-KNIGHT FEDERAL PROSECUTOR battling crooked Wall Streeters and call girls, Eliot Spitzer was known as Mr. Clean. Less than two years after being elected New York's governor, he had a new nickname: Client 9. In March investigators linked him to a Manhattan prostitution ring, forcing Spitzer—a married father of three teenage daughters—to confess to patronizing high-priced escorts (referred to as Client 9 on wiretaps, he apparently spent $4,300 for two hours with "Kristen," later identified as aspiring singer Ashley Dupré, 23). Spitzer's wife, Silda, 50, stood gamely by his side at his March 12 resignation; despite rumors that their marriage was ruined, they celebrated their 21st wedding anniversary together in October. Still, his sudden fall and public humiliation were, said friends, enormously costly for the couple. "It was the loss of the future they invested in," said one friend. "People really believed the White House was in store for them."

The Big Fall

OMG– They're 50!

This could be the greatest AARP annual party ever!

OKAY, SO MAYBE TONIGHT HE'S going to party like it's $4.99 (plus tax for the early-bird supper). And maybe lately she's more vintage than virgin. And maybe Michael Jackson pops ibuprofen after a hard day of moonwalking. Point is, these '80s icons have reached the half-century mark and they are, more or less, still rockin'. Prince, for instance, played at the 2007 Super Bowl and put out a new book and CD this year. Madonna retired the cone bra but managed to sign a new $120 million recording deal in 2007—and seems to weigh *less* than she did in her 20s. And MJ marked the 25th anniversary of his biggest hit by issuing *Thriller 25* (occasionally he's in the news for nonmusical reasons, too). Which all goes to show rock and roll keeps you young—though if you do catch Prince in a little red Corvette, it may be a sign of midlife crisis.

Prince

1985

Madonna

Michael Jackson

1984

Early '70s

BILL IDOL SONGS

OF THE BEST

HMV Price £7.99

Now *That's* Recycling...

I'S HARD TO GET YOUR face on a record album (especially now that they aren't made anymore). But it's easy—as "sleevefacing," the latest goofy Internet trend, proved—to put an album face on *you*. Some, like this knockout Billy Idol shot (above) posted on Flickr, are the product of planning; others less so. When Gabriel Kuo found an Elton John LP at a record shop, he realized his girlfriend was wearing almost the same shirt. "We had to do it," he said of their contribution to sleeveface art.

She Gave Up $1 Million!

FIRST KATHY COX WON A MILLION bucks on *Are You Smarter Than a 5th Grader?* (she knew Queen Victoria was the longest-reigning British monarch). Then she gave it all away to three special-needs schools in Georgia, where she is state schools superintendent. "We've got credit card debt, car payments and a mortgage," said Cox, 44, whose husband has a home-building business. "But this was for the students." Turns out that keeping the money wouldn't have made much difference—in November the Coxes filed for bankruptcy, listing $3.5 million in liabilities. The schools, it seems, will still get their million.

I'm All Ears. Really.

COULD IT BE . . . SATAN? NO, IT'S just Yoda, a four-eared cat who was minding his own business, doing normal cat stuff, until Glenn Olsen, the son of his owners, Valerie and Ted Rock of Downers Gover, Ill., posted pictures of him on a photography Web site. Yoda, 2, who has a rare but otherwise harmless genetic defect that results in split earlobes, became an Internet sensation, drawing media interest from as far away as England and Australia—which, as so often happens with celebrities, made it more difficult to interact with true fans. "We don't want anyone to steal him," said Valerie, who decided to keep Yoda indoors for a while.

IN REMEMBRANCE Mourners placed stuffed animals outside the crime scene. Said *Idol* judge Randy Jackson: "The world is an ugly place right now."

Jennifer Hudson's Nightmare

HER RISE TO STARDOM WAS STRAIGHT OUT OF *CINDER-ella*—then the fairy tale was shattered. On Oct. 24 police found singer Jennifer Hudson's mother, Darnell, 57, and brother Jason, 29, shot to death in the house where Hudson grew up in a crime-ridden Chicago neighborhood. Three days later, her sister Julia's son Julian, 7, was found shot in the head in an abandoned SUV. It fell to Hudson, 27—an *American Idol* finalist and Oscar winner for *Dreamgirls*—to identify her nephew's body. "She was the leader," her spokesman told PEOPLE. "Everyone in the room was crying. But they're a strong family." Police arrested Julia's estranged husband, William "Flex" Balfour, 27, for a parole violation, calling him a "person of interest." As of Nov. 17 authorities had not named a suspect. "Jennifer will pull through this," said Hudson's *Idol* castmate LaToya London. "She's a fighter."

> In her time Jennifer will pull through this. She's a fighter "

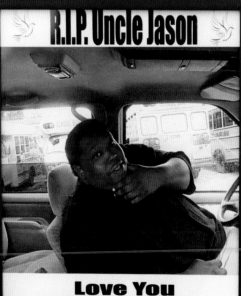

R.I.P. Uncle Jason

Love You Nephew Boo

THE VICTIMS
"Her mom was her rock," a friend says of Jennifer Hudson (with sister Julia, nephew Julian and mother Darnell in '06). Above: Hudson's brother Jason.

Where's Caylee?

ON JULY 15 CINDY ANTHONY CALLED OR-lando police to report her granddaughter Caylee missing. Caylee's mom, Casey, 22, told a shocking story: She claimed she gave the 3-year-old to a babysitter a month before, hadn't seen her since and hadn't bothered to call police. As authorities began a massive search, ugly revelations came thick and fast: Police found no evidence that the alleged babysitter, whom Casey identified as Zenaida Fernandez-Gonzalez, even existed; before Caylee's disappearance, her mom had gone online to do searches on chloroform and on missing children; tests showed evidence of

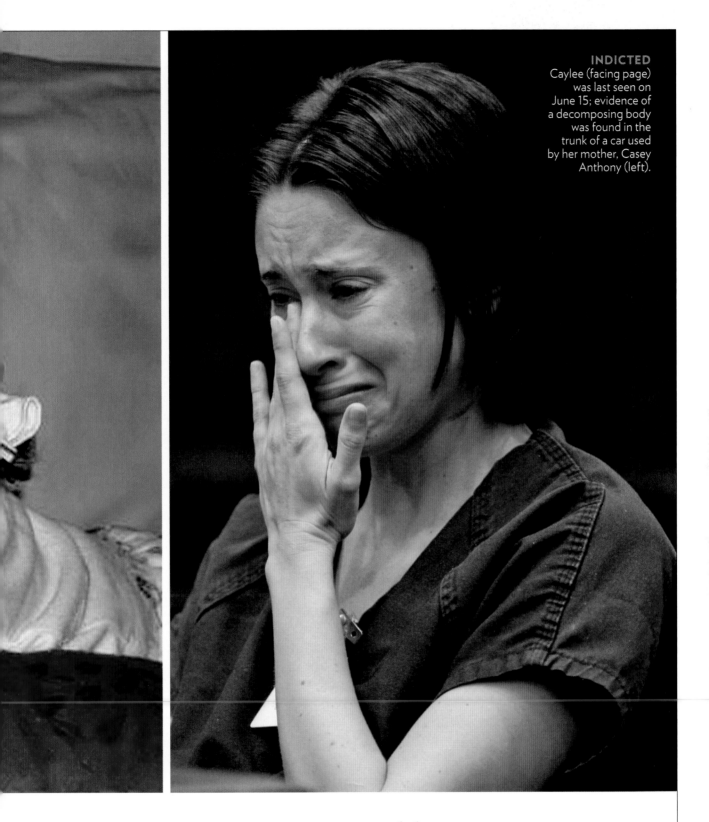

chloroform in the trunk of Casey's car; and Casey, a single mom, had complained to her boyfriend about being chained down by "the little snot head." Additionally—and chillingly—shortly after the last known sighting of Caylee, Casey borrowed a shovel from neighbors. On Oct. 14 Casey was indicted for murder.

" She has given us no meaningful cooperation whatsoever "
—CAPT. ANGELO NIEVES, ORANGE COUNTY SHERIFF'S DEPT.

Royals
in Uniform

Harry serves in Afghanistan, and William gets his wings

ON PATROL
William sent Harry a letter saying he thought their mom, the late Princess Diana, would have been very proud of him.

"ENGLAND EXPECTS THAT EVERY MAN will do his duty," Admiral Nelson famously signaled at the Battle of Trafalgar. Two centuries later the royal family was still at it. In a secret maneuver in which many in the press agreed to keep mum, Prince Harry, 23, served 10 weeks in Afghanistan before being outed—and put in danger—by a tattling Web site. "I would like to still be out there with the guys," he said, disappointed. "This is about as normal as I'm ever going to get." In England, Prince William, 25, received his wings as a pilot in the Royal Air Force, with girlfriend Kate Middleton looking on. Life, of course, was not all about the martial arts. Back home Harry (above) got a laugh out of William's robed appearance at a ceremony; in Mustique in August, William, with Kate, seemed to enjoy a chance to get out of uniform.

FLY BOY
In April, William (with Kate Middleton) received his RAF wings, as three generations of Windsors had done before him.

Tween Madness
Swallowed by the wail: Girls go crazy for the Jonas Brothers & friends

SELENA GOMEZ
"I'm a Texas girl at heart"

SHE'S THE TOMBOY TEEN wizard on the Disney hit *Wizards of Waverly Place*, dates Nick Jonas and keeps getting called "the next Miley Cyrus." If that happens, she'll have to thank a large purple dinosaur, on whose show she got her start. Says Gomez, 16: "I learned everything from Barney."

THE JONAS BROTHERS
(from left) Nick, 16, Kevin, 21, and Joe, 19

TEEN POPS NEWEST, CUTest 2,000-lb. gorillas? That—as any parent of an 11-year-old girl knows—would be the Jonas Brothers, who turned musical hooks, mop tops and a gig as megastar Miley Cyrus's opening act into a showbiz jackpot. So far? Millions of albums sold, an upcoming TV show and oceans of screaming tweens. "It's crazy when police have to hold back girls," says Joe. "But awesome."

THE NAKED BROTHERS BAND
Mock-rock for the small set

THEY AREN'T REALLY naked, but they *are* brothers: Nat, 13, and Alex, 10, whose band is the focus of Nickelodeon's monster hit, are the children of actress Polly Draper (*thirtysomething*) and Michael Wolff, who was musical director for *The Arsenio Hall Show*.

THEIR 30-YEAR MARRIAGE SEEMED ROCK-SOLID, having survived the death of a son, a diagnosis of incurable cancer and two failed presidential campaigns. But the Edwardses faced another agonizing challenge last August when John, 55, confessed to having a "short" affair with Rielle Hunter, 44, a onetime aide. "I am ashamed of my conduct," he said in a statement—though friends close to Elizabeth say his confession has not spared her enormous pain and upheaval. Her choice to stay with her husband has not been easy, they say, but is guided by the reality that her cancer may deprive her three children of a mother. After retreating for three months, Elizabeth, 59, resumed her public advocacy of health-care reform. John canceled all appearances until after the election.

John
Edwards

THE OTHER WOMAN
Rielle Hunter shot films for Edwards' Web site in '06. Last February she gave birth to a daughter. Edwards offered to take a paternity test, but Hunter, citing privacy, refused to allow it.

A Happy Couple Vanish

LIFE WAS SWEET FOR JOHN AND Elizabeth Calvert, especially on their yacht in a marina they owned on Hilton Head Island, S.C. Then on March 4 they disappeared—and police still don't know what happened to them. "It's possible I was the last person who saw them," Dennis Gerwing, a business associate, told PEOPLE just two days before he was found dead on March 11, an apparent suicide. Did Gerwing embezzle money from the Calverts? Did he kill them? Police have yet to crack the case. Meanwhile friends still mourn the couple. Said one: "They were living their dream."

'Any Second It Can All Be Gone'

WHEN THE PLANE WAS ON THE RUNway, I took my shoes off and fell asleep," DJ AM, 35, recalled later. The next thing he remembered was "us crashing into something. . . . The plane was engulfed in flames. I remember thinking it was like *Miami Vice*, where a car is on fire and you run before the gas tank explodes." AM and former blink-182 drummer Travis Barker, 33, who had performed together that night in Columbia, S.C., escaped the burning fuselage through a wall of fire; each suffered extensive second- and third-degree burns. Barker's personal assistant, bodyguard and the pilot and copilot died.

AM, born Adam Goldstein, was sedated and airlifted to a burn center, where he awoke two days later. He endured numerous skin grafts and long sessions in a hyperbaric oxygen chamber. "Why did I live?" he asked himself. "I don't question it. All I know is I'm thankful I'm still here."

AFTERMATH
AM (above, with Barker, and, left, after the crash) says he won't board a small plane again like the one that crashed (below): "Too scary."

A Victim Speaks

SHAWN HORNBECK WAS KID-napped in 2002 and—in what seemed a miracle—found alive in 2007, living with his abductor. But why had he never tried to escape? In October, speaking publicly for the first time, Hornbeck, now 17, said he had been bound to a bed for a month and sexually abused; when his abductor began to strangle him, Hornbeck begged for his life and promised never to leave. "People see it in their power to judge me," he said. "They don't know what I went through. They weren't there."

Freed At Last

THE PLAN WAS STRAIGHT out of Hollywood—and, astoundingly, it worked. On July 2 Colombian commandos, disguised as rebels and humanitarian workers, persuaded real rebels, with their captives, to board a helicopter—then pounced, freeing Ingrid Betancourt, 46, a former Colombian senator, and three Americans: Thomas Howes, 55; Keith Stansel, 43; and Marc Gonsalves, 36. All had been hostages for more than five years. Seeing her family again after years of torture and hardship, said Betancourt, was "like an explosion of happiness."

REUNITED
Betancourt (above, with children Melanie and Lorenzo), held six years (left), described her captors as "monstrous."

Brother, Can You Spare A Billion?

Risky loans and tanking stocks trigger an economic meltdown—and turn "CEO" into a four-letter word

THE SINGULAR FEATURE of the great crash of 1929," economist John Kenneth Galbraith wrote long ago, "was that the worst continued to worsen." Yeah, we know the feeling. Thanks to reckless lenders, greedy CEOs and a free market that, it turns out, is *really* expensive, the stock market teetered like a giant Ponzi scheme and plunged the U.S. economy into crisis. Endless foreclosures, massive layoffs, mammoth bailouts, big companies nearly going belly-up—will unprecedented billions from the government avert *The Great Depression: Part Deux*? Or—*gulp*—will the worst get worse?

Five Who Got Rich

Angelo Mozilo
Ex-CEO, Countrywide Financial
Took home $360 million in 2005-2007, even as the giant mortgage lender reported billions in losses.

Martin Sullivan
Ex-CEO, AIG
Made $25 million from 2005 to 2007, including $153K for car and parking, before AIG's bailout.

LOSING HOUSE AND HOME
By one estimate, banks and loan investors owned 826,200 foreclosed homes through August of 2008—up from 343,500 in 2007. At the same time, the 10 best-paid CEOs in the U.S. made more than half a billion dollars last year.

Richard Fuld
Ex-CEO, Lehman Brothers
Earned at least $350 million since 2000; agreed to resign after the bank filed for Chapter 11 in September.

Daniel Mudd
Ex-CEO, Fannie Mae
He hauled in some $28 million since 2000 before the Feds took over the beleaguered company.

Stanley O'Neal
Ex-CEO, Merrill Lynch
Earned $161 million in exit pay before his firm was taken over by Bank of America.

The Global Family
Around the World with the Jolie-Pitts

New Orleans
October 6
Mom with Zahara (left),
Shiloh . . . and Cheetos.

Mammoth, Calif.
February 16
Pax and Dad ride
the wild tubes at
a snow park.

New York City
October 4
Zahara, Maddox, Pax
and Mom shop for art
supplies in the big city.

Mugello, Italy
June 1
Maddox and Pop, off to
the races at the Italian
motorcycling Grand Prix.

HEATHER LOCKLEAR
The former *Melrose Place* star, 47, who in June had sought treatment for anxiety and depression at an Arizona facility, was arrested for suspicion of DUI on Sept. 27 near Santa Barbara, Calif. On Nov. 17, a misdemeanor charge was formally entered; arraignment was set for Jan. 26. If convicted, Locklear faces penalties ranging from a fine to up to six months in county jail.

Trouble

For some celebs, 2008 brought a court date, rehab—or jail time

KIEFER SUTHERLAND (DUI)
The *24* star spent 48 days—including Christmas—in jail for a second DUI conviction and violating probation.

MISCHA BARTON (Suspicion of DUI)
Arrested Dec. 27, 2007, in L.A., the actress pleaded no contest on April 10 and was ordered to attend alcohol education classes.

RICHIE SAMBORA (Suspicion of DUI)
The Bon Jovi guitarist was arrested on March 25. He later pleaded no contest and was sentenced to three years probation and ordered to attend alcohol education classes.

RYAN O'NEAL (Suspicion of drug possession)
The actor, 67, was arrested with his son Redmond on Sept. 17 and later charged with felony drug possession. He is to appear in court in early 2009.

JOSH BROLIN (Interfering with police)
Arrested July 12 in connection with an alleged bar brawl while filming in Shreveport. The actor was due in court in December.

Seeking Treatment

DAVID DUCHOVNY
The actor entered rehab for sex addiction and separated from his wife, actress Téa Leoni.

KIRSTEN DUNST
In February the actress checked into a treament center to deal with depression.

SHIA LABEOUF (Misdemeanor DUI)
The *Indiana Jones* star was arrested July 27 after an accident at 2:30 a.m. in L.A. Charges were later dropped for "insufficient evidence."

AMY WINEHOUSE
(Suspicion of possessing drugs) The troubled singer, who had entered drug rehab earlier in the year, was arrested on May 7 after she was caught on video smoking what appeared to be crack. Charges were dropped after police could not determine what, in fact, she was smoking. Two Brits later pleaded guilty to offering to supply Winehouse with drugs.

> " Suri is talking up a
> storm; she has a
> strong personality "
>
> —A FAMILY FRIEND

Suri Turns 2

SHE SEEMS TO HAVE SKIPPED THE TER-
rible twos and gone straight to the Adorable-All-
the-Times. "She's as beautiful as they come—
happy and friendly," a family friend says of Suri Cruise,
who had her second birthday in April—and is, at least,
clearly in the running for the coveted Hollywood's Most
Precious Pipsqueak title. So what if her famous folks
had a so-so year (Tom Cruise's film studio is struggling;
Katie Holmes' latest movie, *Mad Money*, flopped)?
The couple, say friends, are positively smitten with
Suri, who loves ladybugs, dresses and Rihanna—but
holds her own during play dates with neighbor David
Beckham's three boys. "She is so magical," Holmes told
PEOPLE. "I'm feeling so lucky to have her."

YES SURI! "Tom and Katie dote on her," a source
says of the much-traveled tyke (in L.A. in March,
above, left; with Cruise in Colorado on July 4, inset;
and in N.Y.C. in August with Holmes, above).

"I WAS SO MAD I WAS JUST shaking," Christina Applegate said about her breast cancer diagnosis. But the Emmy-nominated star of *Samantha Who?*, who grew even more concerned when she discovered she carried the breast cancer gene BRCA1, wasted little time getting a double mastectomy. "I wanted to be rid of it," she told *Good Morning America*. "I didn't want to go back to the doctor every four months." Applegate, 37, whose mother battled breast cancer twice, had begun getting mammograms at age 30 but credited a doctor-ordered MRI with detecting the cancer and saving her life. The actress is already looking at the bright side of reconstructive surgery. "I'm going to have cute boobs," she said, "till I'm 90."

Christina Applegate

CELEB SURVIVORS
Christina Applegate joined fellow breast cancer survivors Sheryl Crow and Melissa Etheridge last September at the *Stand Up to Cancer* TV special that raised funds for research.

Lindsay Monroe

AS IF THE DRAMA OF HER OWN life—parties, romances, rehab, family drama and a new relationship with DJ Samantha Ronson (right)—were not enough, Lindsay Lohan, 22, has developed a habit of dressing up as other celebs. On and in magazines past, she has appeared as Ann-Margret (ENTERTAINMENT WEEKLY), Elizabeth Taylor (*Interview*) and Liza Minnelli (*Premiere*); this year, for *New York* magazine, she channeled Marilyn Monroe, in the famous nude series photographed by Ben Stern in 1962. "I looked at it as art," said Lindsay's mother, Dina, who added that Lindsay prepped for the bare-all session by doing 250 crunches.

"I Feel So Embarrassed"

UNDER FIRE FOR CONTROVERSIAL PHOTOS IN *VANITY FAIR* AND ON THE INTERNET, TEEN SUPERSTAR MILEY CYRUS SPEAKS OUT: "I AM NOT PERFECT."

Miley's Miscues

COMES THE TIME, IT SEEMS, IN EVERY tween star's life when regrettable photos appear. For squeaky-clean *Hannah Montana* superstar Miley Cyrus, 16, April offered a double whammy: Pix of the teen cuddling with a boy and showing her bra appeared on the Web, and a sexy shirtless image (inset) taken for *Vanity Fair* began to circulate. Singed by criticism, Miley apologized to fans ("I feel so embarrassed") and said she would trust "my family and my faith" to help her make better choices in the future.

Weddings

Elaborate? Intimate? In a chapel?
On the beach? No matter; 'tis love makes
a wedding perfect

ELLEN
DeGENERES
and PORTIA
DE ROSSI

THEY DO!
Getting married "is not
something we've ever
taken for granted,"
said de Rossi (with
DeGeneres, both in
Zac Posen designs).
"That we get to do this,
it means a lot."

AFTER SCRAPPING PLANS FOR A LARGER AFFAIR, THE
couple settled on an intimate ceremony attended by just 19 of
their closest friends and relatives. "It was really important for
us that the wedding be something we would enjoy," said de Rossi, 35.
"The love we felt from the people surrounding us, and the love we have
for each other, made it the most beautiful and emotional day." As for
her bride, "what can I say? I'm the luckiest girl in the world," declared
DeGeneres, 50, who proposed after California's Supreme Court ruled
a previous ban on gay marriage to be unconstitutional. At the reception—which featured an all-vegan menu and a surprise performance by
one of de Rossi's favorite singers, Joshua Radin—the couple danced to
their favorite love song, Stevie Wonder's "Ribbon in the Sky." "It's just
one of those things where you know you found your soulmate," said the
elated talk show host. "That you were born to be with this person."

MARIAH
CAREY
and NICK
CANNON
April 30, 2008

SWEPT AWAY
"I never felt a love
like this was in the
cards for me," said
Carey (in a Nile Cmylo
dress and Christian
Louboutin heels).

JUST WEEKS AFTER THEY STARTED DATing, the surprise couple shocked many of their friends and family with an oceanside wedding at Carey's Bahamian estate. "In our minds, it was a love-at-first-sight thing," said Cannon. "Since we've been together, we've been inseparable." The actor-comedian, 27, proposed on April 25 with a 17-carat pink diamond ring created by Jacob & Co.'s Jacob Arabo. Five days later, the pair were exchanging vows at sunset in front of a dozen guests. "The whole wedding was really beautiful and sweet," said Carey, 39. "Being there with loved ones under the sky . . . it was a spiritual moment." As for starting a family, "it's part of the whole purpose of getting married," said the singer. "I'd just want our children to have the best childhood and upbringing they possibly could."

ASHLEE
SIMPSON
and PETE
WENTZ
May 17, 2008

FOR THEIR WHIMSICAL ROCK AND ROLL wedding, the couple took their cues from *Alice in Wonderland*: The wedding cake was in the shape of a Mad Hatter-style top hat, guests sipped from miniature bottles of tequila labeled "Drink Me!" and the pair's English bulldog Hemingway served as ring bearer. Said Fall Out Boy bassist Pete, 28: "We wanted people to feel like they stepped into a topsy-turvy world." It was emotional too, with Ashlee, 23, and her big sister Jessica—who also served as her maid of honor—sobbing as the ceremony got under way. Guests like Nicole Richie and Joel Madden partied in a tent in the backyard of Simpson's parents' Encino, Calif., home, which had been filled with 10,000 roses. "I was skipping around all night," said Ashlee. "Like, 'Oh my God, I'm a wife!'" But wait, there's more: Later in the year, the newlyweds welcomed a son, Bronx Mowgli Wentz, born Nov. 20.

OPTING FOR AN OUTDOOR TEXAS WED-ding rather than a White House affair, the President's daughter made the most of the Bush family's beloved Crawford ranch. After a lakeside ceremony attended by 200 guests, Jenna, 26, and Henry, 30—who met when they both worked at George Bush's 2004 reelection headquarters—retreated to a fishing dock for a private toast. At the reception, President Bush danced with his daughter to "You Are So Beautiful" before a high-energy set by musician Tyrone Smith and his band. "Super T," implored the new Jenna Hager, "pick it up!" The father of the bride partied until 1 a.m. and declared it "an awfully special weekend. Our little girl Jenna married a really good guy."

JENNA
BUSH *and*
HENRY
HAGER
May 10, 2008

CHRIS EVERT
and GREG NORMAN
June 28, 2008

H E MAY BE NICKNAMED "THE GREAT WHITE SHARK" ON THE links, but when Greg Norman saw his Carolina Herrera-clad bride walk down the aisle, the shark got teary. "All I could think was, 'Wow, she looks stunning!'" said Norman, 53, who wed tennis legend Evert, also 53, at the One & Only Ocean Club in the Bahamas. "Time stood still and everything else disappeared. We were two people becoming one, and it was beautiful." The couple have five children from previous marriages, each of whom poured individual glasses of sand into one bowl to signify the merging of the two families. "Seeing them embrace us really warmed my heart," said Evert. To cap off the evening, the newlyweds jumped into the pool—fully clothed. "Thank heaven I had changed out of my wedding gown," said Evert. "It was the best!"

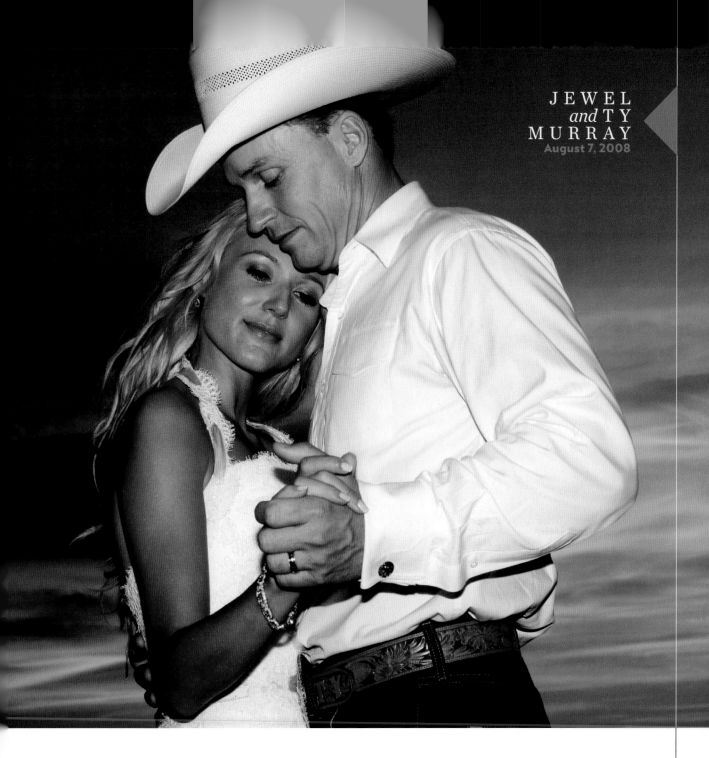

AFTER 10 YEARS OF TOGETHERNESS, THE Alaska-bred singer, 34, and the rodeo star, 38, were more than ready to make it official. During their self-written vows, "Neither of us cried," said Jewel. "We were happy!" Having chosen to elope to the Bahamas, the couple called their families afterward to break the news. Why elope? "That's what marriage is," said Murray. "Just me and her." During a surprise fireworks display at the Cove Atlantis (a gift from the resort), "we danced and held hands," said Jewel, who went barefoot in a Monique Lhuillier gown. The very private affair—only pals Jason Freese, who officiated, and his wife, Amy, attended—"was picture perfect," said Murray, who wore his signature jeans and cowboy hat. The newlyweds dined on Bahamian lobster and chocolate bento boxes, along with a cake that featured a cowboy-and-bride cake topper that Jewel found online. "To elope and pull off the wedding quietly made it magical," said the singer, adding, "We're ready to start a family."

GEORGE TAKEI *and* BRAD ALTMAN
September 14, 2008

MR. SULU WAS BEAMING. After waiting 21 years for the planets to align and gay marriage to be made legal in California, *Star Trek* costar George Takei, 71, and his longtime partner and manager, Brad Altman, 54, wed in a moving but lighthearted ceremony that included a Buddhist priest, a Scottish bagpiper and, as maid of honor, *Trek*'s Commander Uhura, actress Nichelle Nichols. Table cards read, "May Sweet Equality Live Long and Prosper."

WHEN YOU'VE GOT seven kids—three hers, four his—things happen. Country singer Sara Evans, 37, and her fiancé, radio host Jay Barker, 36, missed their respective bachelor and bachelorette parties and spent the evening in the ER because they feared her daughter had appendicitis (it was a false alarm). The wedding itself, in which the couple vowed to love each other's children as their own, went off without a hitch. One highlight: a song called "Bless the Broken Road," performed by a Barker friend. "The words say, 'God blessed the broken road that led me straight to you,'" said Evans, who, like Barker, divorced last year. "That's so true and so fitting for us."

IVANA
TRUMP *and*
ROSSANO
RUBICONDI
April 12, 2008

THE GROOM WORE WHITE BUT THE bride wore pink—and lots of it. At Ivana Trump's nearly $3 million wedding to Italian model-actor Rossano Rubicondi, 36, the 59-year-old socialite had three different pastel gowns for her bash at Mar-a-Lago, the Palm Beach club owned by her ex Donald Trump. After descending a butterfly staircase, Ivana exchanged vows with Rubicondi, who entered to the *Rocky* theme song and yelled, "Finally!" to a happy roar from the 400 guests. As for the 23-year age gap? "I am very much in love," said Trump of her fourth husband. "I have so much energy, an older man cannot keep up with me!" Perhaps; at any rate, there were certainly problems. In December, Trump revealed that she and Rubicondi had separated months earlier.

FAMOUSLY TIGHT-LIPPED ABOUT THEIR SIX-year relationship, Jay-Z, 39, and Beyoncé, 27 (in L.A.), pulled off a top-secret wedding at the groom's luxurious Tribeca penthouse with a close circle of 40 friends and family. "It was a very emotional wedding . . . and very spiritual," said a guest. The vows were stream-lined, but the party went on all night as guests danced under a white tent erected in the basketball-court-size living room. For months the couple refused to confirm their nuptials, but in September Beyoncé finally showed the world her whopping $5 million, 18-carat-diamond ring.

KATHARINE McPHEE *and* NICK COKAS
February 2, 2008

KATHARINE McPHEE'S favorite memory of her wedding to producer Nick Cokas? The moment when the doors to the Beverly Hills Presbyterian Church swung open. "I had been holding on to my dad, trying not to cry," she says. "Then the doors opened, and I was blown away." The *American Idol* winner, in a Manuel Mota gown and $250,000 worth of borrowed Neil Lane jewels, and her husband, 42, said "I do" before 305 guests, including *Idol* pal Kellie Pickler, a bridesmaid. Said McPhee, 23: "I was so emotional and moved by the whole thing."

JIMMY FALLON *and* NANCY JUVONEN
December 22, 2007

IT'S ALMOST A MOVIE: ACTOR is cast in romantic comedy, falls in love with and marries—the producer? That was the trajectory for *Saturday Night Live* alum Jimmy Fallon, 33, who on Dec. 22 married Nancy Juvonen, 40, coproducer of 2005's *Fever Pitch,* in which Fallon costarred with Drew Barrymore. Fallon announced the couple would be taking each other's names, and henceforth he would be known as Jancy Falvonen.

WHEN I WAS A LITTLE GIRL, it was all about the princess fairy tale," Jessica Alba told PEOPLE early in the year. "But life is changing every day, and I'm just going with it." Go with it she did: The actress, eight months pregnant, and her fiancé, producer Cash Warren, 31, walked into the Beverly Hills Municipal Court about noon on May 19 and were married, with joy but little fanfare, by a court staffer. Three weeks later the couple became parents to a little girl, Honor Marie. Said Alba, 27, of her new life: "I feel super-blessed."

Hello, Baby!

Christina Aguilera,
Clay Aiken, Matthew
McConaughey and
more say welcome
to the family

MEETING MAX
"The connection was incredible," Aguilera says of the moment she first held her son. "You can't believe the love you feel."

CLAY AIKEN *and* PARKER FOSTER AIKEN
August 8, 2008
6 lbs. 2 oz.

THE FORMER *AMERICAN Idol* runner-up, 29, and his friend, music producer Jaymes Foster, 50, welcomed son Parker Foster Aiken at 8:08 on a summer morning at a North Carolina hospital. Parker, which is Aiken's stepfather's surname, measured 19 in. long. On Aiken's blog, the singer gushed, "The little man is healthy, happy and as loud as his daddy." Within a month, however, Parker began vomiting all day. The baby was diagnosed with pyloric stenosis, an intestinal condition which complicates digestion. He underwent surgery to correct the problem, and emerged healthy once more. "It was a reality check," said Aiken. One that led him to take his role as a father even more seriously, and acknowledge, for the first time publicly, that he is gay. "I cannot raise a child to lie or to hide things," Aiken told PEOPLE. "I wasn't raised that way, and I'm not going to raise a child to do that." As for Aiken's hopes for the child's future, "I want to raise him in an environment that is accepting and allowing him to be happy. I have no idea if he'll be gay or straight. . . . It's already probably up inside the code there—you know what I mean?"

CHRISTINA AGUILERA *and* MAX LIRON BRATMAN
January 12, 2008   6 lbs. 2 oz.

'M HEAD OVER HEELS IN LOVE," SAID THE singer, cupping her little boy's head and watching his tiny fingers reach up to his mom's cheek. "He's completely changed my life." He is Max Liron Bratman, the first child for Aguilera, 27, and her husband, Jordan Bratman, 30, a music exec. And he has completely mesmerized his mom. "When he's breast-feeding, I just sit there and stare at him," said Aguilera. "I'm in awe of this little miracle." Dad was impressed too. "He's a product of our love," said Bratman, who married Aguilera in Napa Valley in 2005. And as for Max Liron (combined, his Latin first name and Hebrew middle name roughly translate to "our greatest song"), Aguilera said he is a "sweet, mellow baby."

I cannot raise a child to lie or to hide things. I wasn't raised that way, and I'm not going to raise a child to do that "

A FAMILY BEGINS
"I think this is always going to be remembered by me as the most magical time," said Lopez.

KATE & OWEN: THEIR ON-AGAIN ROMANCE

People

ONLY IN People
JENNIFER LOPEZ

TWIN BLISS!

WORLD EXCLUSIVE Intimate photos at home (and in the nursery!) with Jennifer Lopez, Marc Anthony and babies Max and Emme

JENNIFER LOPEZ, MARC ANTHONY *and* MAX *and* EMME
February 22, 2008
5 lbs. 13 oz.
5 lbs. 7 oz.

"YOU HEAR PEOPLE SAY THIS ALL THE TIME, BUT IT'S NOT UNTIL you experience it yourself that you can put it into your own words. Your heart is connected to them," Jennifer Lopez told PEOPLE just weeks after giving birth to Emme and Max, her children with singer Marc Anthony, 40. "It feels like there's a string from my chest to theirs." Her love was so intense, Lopez says, that she stayed awake the first three days after giving birth "because I just wanted to keep staring at them." Adds her husband: "You have all these amazing little moments. It's just perfect now." At long last; Lopez, 39, had wanted children for years. "You start getting older, you think to yourself, 'Maybe [having kids] is just not meant for me,'" Lopez said. "I knew there was nothing wrong with me. I knew that I could."

PERHAPS IT'S A SMIDGEN EARLY TO CALL little Brody Jo Hamilton a super athlete, but she's got potential. Mom, Gabrielle Reece, 38, is a former volleyball star. Dad, Laird Hamilton, 44, is a world-class surfer. The 6'3" Reece was back in shape a mere six weeks after giving birth via C-section. "I stayed fit during pregnancy, so my body went back quickly," she says. The family, including daughter Viola, 4, like to hit the beach near their Hawaii home. Notes Hamilton, who also has a daughter, Izabela, from a previous marriage: "I always wanted to be surrounded by women."

GABRIELLE
REECE,
LAIRD
HAMILTON
and BRODY JO
January 1, 2008
8 lbs. 2 oz.

MATTHEW McCONAUGHEY, CAMILA ALVES *and* LEVI ALVES

July 7, 2008   7 lbs. 4 oz.

MALIBU HAS A NEW LITTLE SURFER DUDE! THIS summer Matthew McConaughey and his girlfriend Camila Alves welcomed their baby boy at a Santa Monica hospital. McConaughey, 39, had previously announced the pregnancy on his Web site, proclaiming, "We are stoked!" The actor and Alves, 25, have been catching rays from California to the Bahamas since they started dating in '06. Expect Junior to embrace their laid-back life. "No doubt about it," McConaughey has said. "My kid will dance. He will be on the beach, and he will be taking hikes with a wild bandanna on." Righteous, dude.

BABY LOVE Alves (with McConaughey) holds a sleepy Levi.

JAMIE
LYNN
SPEARS *and*
MADDIE
BRIANN
ALDRIDGE
June 19, 2008
7 lbs. 11 oz.

SHE WAS ONLY 17, AND NOT MARRIED, BUT BRITNEY'S little sister Jamie Lynn Spears brought joy to the family the morning she gave birth to Maddie Briann, her child with fiancé Casey Aldridge, 19. "For once, everyone was together," a family friend told PEOPLE. "This baby could be a turning point in the family." Jamie Lynn, the former Nickelodeon star, showed new signs of maturity after announcing her pregnancy. She earned her GED, got engaged and decorated her new home. Says a friend: "She's taking full responsibility for her own life, making good choices and good decisions."

AMONG THE BENEFITS NICOLE Richie, 26, noticed after the birth of Harlow, her daughter with rocker Joel Madden, 29: "The family has gotten closer. Harlow is really the focus, and everyone has the same goal: to love her and to make her happy." The baby has also brought a change in lifestyle to a woman once known for partying: "I stop doing things for me anymore." And has the baby met Paris Hilton, Nicole's former club mate? "Yeah. They went to the Ivy. Just kidding."

NICOLE
RICHIE
and HARLOW
January 11, 2008
6 lbs. 7 oz.

JODIE SWEETIN *and* ZOIE
April 12, 2008   8 lbs. 7 oz.

THE LIFE OF THE FORMER *FULL HOUSE* star Jodie Sweetin (she played spunky middle child Stephanie) seems to be only rarely lacking for headlines. After the show ended in 1995, she spiraled into a crystal meth addiction that wrecked her first marriage before she entered rehab in 2005. In 2007 she married transportation coordinator Cody Herpin, 31, and last spring gave birth to daughter Zoie. "You look at your baby and think, 'Wow, I did that'—it's really amazing," Sweetin, 26, said shortly after her daughter's arrival. "I can't believe how far I've come. It's amazing to think about how different my life is now." Alas, there are still unexpected bumps: In November Sweetin and Herpin separated after 16 months of marriage.

ANGELINA JOLIE, BRAD PITT *and* KNOX LEON *and* VIVIENNE MARCHELINE
July 12, 2008

THEIRS IS A HAPPY AND—NO kidding!—growing family. On July 12 at a hospital in Nice, France, Angelina Jolie and Brad Pitt—already parents to Maddox, 7, Pax, 4, Zahara, 3, and Shiloh, 2—welcomed twins Knox Léon and Vivienne Marcheline. "I knew they would be premature," Jolie said later, "so when I saw they were big and screaming with healthy lungs, I was at peace." Pitt's reaction at meeting the newcomers? "An awe words fail to describe," he said. Their new life, Jolie added, "is chaos, but we are managing it and having a wonderful time."

NICOLE KIDMAN *and* SUNDAY ROSE

July 7, 2008
6 lbs. 7.5 oz.

WITH HUSBAND Keith Urban at her side, a thrilled Nicole Kidman, 41, welcomed their first child, daughter Sunday Rose. "We feel immensely blessed and grateful to be given this beautiful baby girl," the couple said in a statement to PEOPLE. "She's an absolute delight." The superstar couple maintain a cozy domestic life in Nashville, but the family plan to take to the road in 2009 for Keith's tour.

HALLE BERRY DOESN'T TAKE NO for an answer. After a long struggle to get pregnant—she had almost three dozen negative pregnancy tests—the actress, 41, and her beau, model Gabriel Aubry, 32, finally welcomed a baby girl, Nahla Ariela Aubry, at L.A.'s Cedars-Sinai Medical Center (Nahla means "honeybee" in Arabic). "It didn't matter if it was a boy or a girl, she wanted it to be a surprise," says a friend. "And that girl is going to be gorgeous!" Her mother continued to be: Only six weeks later she stole the show at a Beverly Hills auction in a plunging leopard-print dress.

A FEW MONTHS BEFORE GIVING birth, Jessica Alba had already decided what to bring *to* the hospital. "I'm packing shea butter, scented candles and meditation music," Alba, 27, told PEOPLE. Weeks later, Alba and her husband, Cash Warren, 31, left L.A.'s Cedars-Sinai Medical Center toting more precious cargo: daughter Honor Marie.

ANNE
HATHAWAY
and RAFFAELLO
FOLLIERI

THEIRS WAS A FAIRY-TALE ROMANCE UNTIL the FBI hauled off her Prince Charming. Anne Hathaway, 25, star of *The Devil Wears Prada,* and Raffaello Follieri, 30, a suave and seemingly superwealthy financier, met through a mutual friend and fell madly in love. But this June, Hathaway ended their four-year affair just days before FBI agents arrested Follieri for bilking millions from investors (he pleaded guilty and agreed to serve 4½ years in prison). "I broke up with my Italian boyfriend, and two weeks later he was sent to prison for fraud," Hathaway—initially devastated, say friends—joked when she hosted *Saturday Night Live* in October. "We've all been there, right, ladies?"

Splits

Once, they called it lovely; in 2008,
Madonna and Guy, Shania and Mutt
and other famous couples
called it quits

**Dated
4 years**

MADONNA
and GUY
RITCHIE

Married
7½ years

HOURS AFTER PUBLICLY CONFIRM-
ing the demise of her 7½-year marriage
to Guy Ritchie on Oct. 15, Madonna, 50,
tore through an athletic, two-hour set on her
Sticky & Sweet tour, revealing only a hint of tur-
bulence by dedicating the song "Miles Away"—
which she said was inspired by her director husband—to the "emotionally retarded." But their
marriage, whose latest hurdle was Madonna's
friendship with baseball star Alex Rodriguez,
had run aground long before then. Sources say
the couple fought over adopting son David from
Malawi in 2006, over Kabbalah and over careers
that kept them physically and emotionally dis-
tant. Still, Madonna and Ritchie, at least publicly,
have remained mum. "It's all about protecting
the kids [Lourdes, 12, Rocco, 8, and David, 3] at
this point," Madonna's close friend Ingrid Casa-
res told PEOPLE. Ritchie, who has been shooting
Sherlock Holmes in England, "is throwing himself
into his filmmaking," said a pal.

A NEW FRIEND
Madonna's ongoing
relationship with Alex
Rodriguez "is spiritual and
emotional," says a source.
She introduced the baseball
all-star to Kabbalah and
brought her son David to
watch a Yankee game in
June. "Everyone thinks
A-Rod is the reason they
split—it's not," said a
Madonna pal. The divorce
was "a long time coming."

JOHN
MAYER *and*
JENNIFER
ANISTON

**Dated
5 months**

Rollercoaster Romances

THE EX-*FRIEND*STER AND THE CHATTY soft rocker lit up gossip columns from April to August, when Mayer, 31, pulled the plug. "There's no lying, there's no cheating," he told reporters after the split. "I don't want to waste somebody's time if something's not right." *Ouch.* But then in October, Aniston, 39, signed up for a sequel, dining out—and cuddling up—with her ex. Said one friend: "There's just major chemistry between them."

SARAH SILVERMAN *and* JIMMY KIMMEL

SHE JOKED ABOUT SLEEP-ing with Matt Damon. He had a faux affair with Ben Affleck. Through it all, they seemed perfect for each other, which is why many were shocked when late-night talk show host Kim-mel, 40, and stand-up star Sil-verman, 37, called it quits in July. Neither addressed the breakup except when Silverman, while accepting a Creative Arts Emmy for her Damon video, thanked "Jimmy Kimmel, who broke my heart—oh, who'll always have a *place* in my heart." The real punch line? They reconnected in October and, said a friend, were "on the road back to being together again."

Married
3 years

Dated
5 years

STAR JONES *and* AL REYNOLDS

HER LAVISH 2004 MANHATTAN wedding featured 450 guests, 12 bridesmaids and even corporate sponsors, fulfilling "every single wedding fantasy I ever had," the former *View* cohost, 46, told PEOPLE shortly after her big day. But within two years, there were rumors of strife, and in March she filed for divorce from Reyn-olds, 38, a banker. Jones kept mum about the breakup, but in July Reynolds posted videos on YouTube to deny he was gay and explain, "We started to grow apart."

Married
10 years

BILL
MURRAY
and
JENNIFER
BUTLER
MURRAY

MARRIAGE IS LIKE BUILDING A house," Murray, 57, once told a fan. "Keep the two foundations far apart. If you hold them too close together, they'll collapse." That advice wasn't enough to save his own marriage; in May his wife, Jennifer, 44, filed for divorce, accusing him of adultery, physical abuse and addiction to alcohol and sex. The messy split "was the worst thing that ever happened to me," Murray—who has four sons, ages 7 to 15, with Jennifer—told the AP in October. "I was just dead."

**Dated
2 Years**

I T WAS MUCH "I DO" ABOUT NOTH-
ing: Murphy, 46, and film producer
Edmonds, 40, traded vows in Bora Bora
on New Year's Day and then, just two weeks
later, essentially said, "Never mind." A
couple since 2006, they reportedly had a
screaming match during their honeymoon
and quickly canceled plans for a U.S. wedding (their island ceremony, attended by 25
friends and family, was not legally binding).
The symbolic union reflected the "respect
that we have for one another on a spiritual
level," the ex-couple said in a statement. But
"we have decided to [stay just] friends."

ROBIN WILLIAMS *and* MARSHA WILLIAMS

FRIENDS USED THE SAME WORD over and over: "It's sad"; "They're sad but going on with their lives"; the kids were "sad but okay." Unlike many celebrity splits, the divorce of Robin Williams, 57, and his wife, Marsha, 52, after 19 years of marriage and two children (Zelda, 19, and Cody, 17) offered no public fireworks, bitterness or winner. Friends of Robin's said that, despite the efforts of both partners, the marriage never recovered from the strain caused by his alcohol relapse in 2006 after 20 years of sobriety. Although he put on a brave face—"She's amazing," he said of her support—in the end, said a friend, "the trust was broken."

Married 14 years

Married 19 years

THEY WERE ONE OF MUSIC'S GREAT power couples, until—as Shania Twain's friends tell it—Mutt was a dog. Twain, 43, one of country's biggest stars, and Robert "Mutt" Lange, 60, a legendary and reclusive songwriter and producer, separated in May after 14 years of marriage—shortly after, Twain associates say, the singer discovered that her husband of 14 years was having an affair with her close friend Marie-Anne Thiébaud, 37, who managed the Swiss château the couple called home. "It's a multiple betrayal because it involves all the people around her," said one friend. "She is in absolute, total shock." After the split, Lange and Thiébaud, who herself was going through a divorce, denied the affair. But a source close to Twain insisted, "They are absolutely still together." Twain, accompanied by the couple's son Eja, 7, sought solace with relatives in Canada. "Shania," said a Swiss friend, "absolutely will get through this."

SHANIA
TWAIN
and
ROBERT
"MUTT"
LANGE

HEARTBREAK
Friends say Twain discovered her husband, Mutt Lange (top, left), was having an affair with close pal Thiébaud (right).

FAB FOUR
Let the boys have *Batman*. For many women, the most eagerly awaited movie of 2008 starred Sarah Jessica Parker, Cynthia Nixon, Kristin Davis, Kim Cattrall, great clothes, Manolo Blahniks and a satisfying love story. In the end, *Sex and the City*—the movie—grossed more than $400 million worldwide.

Movies

Carrie gets married
(finally!), those singing
teens return (again!),
but nobody outshines
The Dark Knight

The Dark Knight

BIG BAD BAT
The Riddler couldn't KO Batman, nor could Two-Face. But *Batman and Robin* almost did—the so-so 1997 sequel starring George Clooney could easily have been the Dynamic Duo's last commercial gasp. Then came Christian Bale, first in 2005's stark, dark *Batman Begins* and, this summer, in *The Dark Knight*—whose billion-dollar worldwide box office guaranteed the brooding hero, it would seem, at least a couple more at bats.

HSM3

LETS PUT ON A SHOW—AGAIN!
High School Musical's tireless Troy, Chad and Gabriella were at it again, singing and dancing their way to graduation and, in the series' third installment, more than $200 million at the box office.

MUSICAL STARS
Zac Efron and Vanessa Hudgens, at rest.

Twilight

PALE, PALE LOVE
She's pretty, moody and a teen. He's pretty, moody and a vampire. *Can their love survive?* In *Twilight's* first three days, 1 zillion fans—most of whom had read the Stephenie Meyer novel that inspired it—spent $70 million to find out.

LOVE IN VEIN
Kristen Stewart and
Robert Pattinson resist.

Iron Man

NICE SUIT!
A special-effects
extravaganza for
the 13-year-old boy
in all of us—well,
many of us—the
year's other big
comic-based
movie earned more
than half a billion.

Rock Star

TINA TIME
30 Rock star Fey won Emmys in three major categories—acting, writing and original comedy series—then, for an encore, turned *Saturday Night Live* into must-see TV with a devastatingly funny Sarah Palin impersonation ("I'd like to use one of my lifelines"). Did her Palin bits also score more than 27 million hits on nbc.com? You betcha.

Television
Prime time ran the gamut from Tina Fey's pinpoint parody to *Gossip Girl* and *Mad Men*

HEAVY METAL After the Emmys, Fey had more hardware than Home Depot.

NEXT! In a three-week stretch, *30 Rock*'s guests included Oprah Winfrey (above), Jennifer Aniston (right, as Fey's nutcase pal) and Steve Martin.

Gossip Girl

ALPHA FEMALES
The buzzed-about CW teen drama, starring
(from left) Leighton Meester, Blake Lively and
Taylor Momsen, shone an obsessive light on the
hardships endured by an oft-ignored minority:
the young, rich and drop-dead gorgeous.

Project Runway

SEW EXCITING
In season 4, towering Teuton Heidi Klum (left) said auf Wiedersehen to everyone but Christian Siriano, self-proclaimed "fierce" fashion force.

Mad Men

BESTSELLERS
Scotch, cigarettes, sharp suits and lust helped John Slattery, Jon Hamm (right) and Elisabeth Moss (left) turn AMC's creative newcomer into a retrosexual delight.

Music

SO, OTHER THAN JONAS Brothers mania, what happened in pop, rock, hip and hop? Dinosaurs happily roamed the planet, Hootie had a country hit, and the latest British invasion had no Y chromosomes.

KATY PERRY
Noted for her unique fashion sense as well as her voice, the 24-year-old, who once released a gospel album, scored summer's big hit with the single "I Kissed a Girl."

London Calling

LEONA LEWIS Her monster single "Bleeding Love" is the bestseller of the year.

ESTELLE The hip-hop star's cannily titled "American Boy" became her first U.S. hit.

ADELE Her emotional LP *19* debuted at No. 1 in Britain; an *SNL* appearance gave a big U.S. boost.

Big Tour

STORMIN' OZZIES AC/DC, a band with a 61-year-old lead singer and firsthand memories of the Pleistocene, rocked arenas.

Big Surprise

HOOTIE Y'ALL Darius Rucker, of Hootie and the Blowfish, scored a No. 1 country hit with "Don't Think I Don't Think About It."

Big Lil

HIP-HOP HIT Lil Wayne's album *The Carter III* sold a million copies in one week—tops for 2008.

Best*
in
Show

For Hollywood's top stars, each year is a fashion
marathon, run in high heels, before flashbulbs, on a red
carpet that stretches from L.A. to New York City.
And this year's winners are ...

*and Worst

Eva
Longoria
Parker

The
Oscars
{February 24, 2008}

Penélope Cruz
Chanel Haute Couture

Anne Hathaway
Marchesa

Cameron Diaz
Dior by John Galliano

Jennifer
Garner
Oscar de la Renta

Keri
Russell
Nina Ricci

Amy
Adams
Proenza Schouler

The Emmys

{September 21, 2008}

Brooke Shields

Badgley Mischka

Heidi Klum

Armani Privé

Kyra Sedgwick

L'Wren Scott

Mariska Hargitay

Carolina Herrera

Vanessa Williams

Kevan Hall

Christina Applegate

Reem Acra

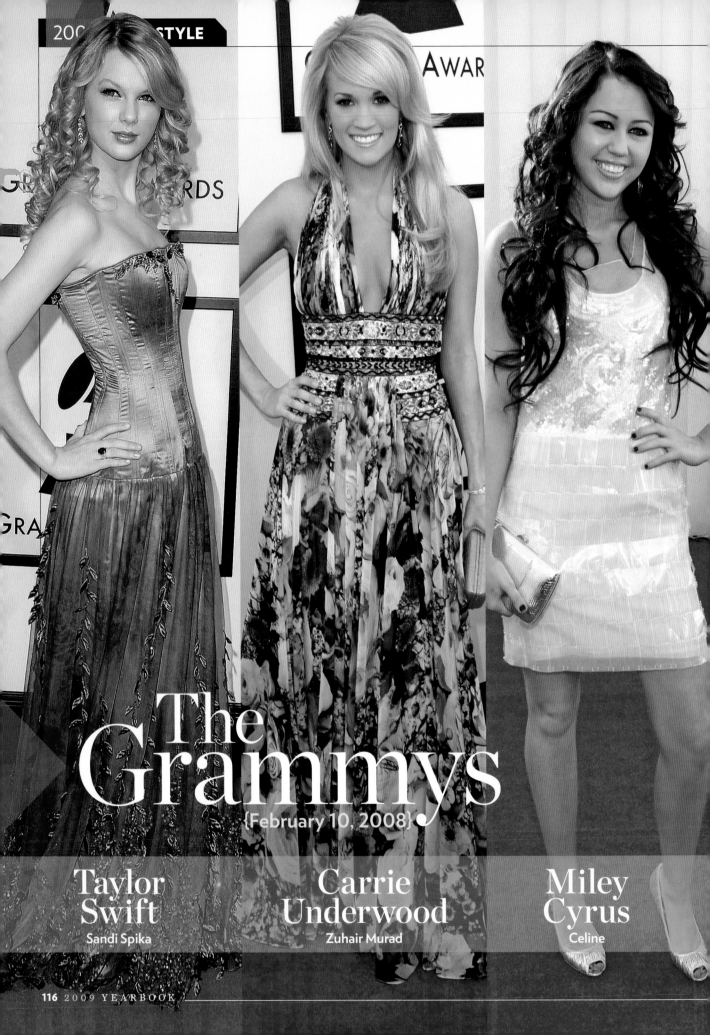

Awar

The Grammys
{February 10, 2008}

Taylor Swift
Sandi Spika

Carrie Underwood
Zuhair Murad

Miley Cyrus
Celine

Beyoncé
Elie Saab

Fergie
Calvin Klein

Rihanna
Zac Posen

SAGs

{January 27, 2008}

Vanessa
Williams

Escada

Ellen
Pompeo

Nina Ricci

January
Jones

Giorgio Armani

Marion Cotillard
Nina Ricci

Kate Hudson
Balmain

America Ferrera
Monique Lhuillier

The Best of the Rest

Angelina Jolie
Max Azria Atelier
At the premiere of *Kung Fu Panda* in Cannes.

Charlize Theron
Atelier Versace
At the premiere of *The Burning Plain* in Venice.

Cate Blanchett
Giorgio Armani Privé
At the premiere of *Blindness* in Cannes.

Jennifer Lopez
Alberta Ferretti
At the Metropolitan Museum of
Art's Costume Institute Gala.

Katie Holmes
Monique Lhuillier
At the premiere of *Lions for Lambs* in L.A.

Carrie Underwood
Naeem Khan
At Movies Rock in L.A.

Worst Dressed

Tilda Swinton
The space-age kimono?

Aubrey O'Day
I made it myself at fashion camp!

Sienna Miller
As flop as a flapper?

Paula Abdul
The Little Mermaid goes to a bullfight?

Solange Knowles
Missing accessory: the kitchen sink?

Lucy Liu
It's a shawl! It's a cape! It's MEGAPUFF!

MAIN ATTRACTION
The actor (backstage in *Baby Want a Kiss* in 1964) first made his name on Broadway.

'08 Farewell

Saying goodbye to the great Paul Newman,
Charlton Heston, Suzanne Pleshette, Bernie Mac,
Tim Russert, George Carlin and more

PAUL
NEWMAN
1925–2008
SEPTEMBER 26

"I'D LIKE TO BE REMEMBERED AS A GUY WHO TRIED," Paul Newman once said. "Tried to be a part of his times, tried to help people communicate with one another, tried to find some decency in his own life, tried to extend himself as a human being. . . . You've got to try, that's the main thing."

He succeeded, spectacularly—while maintaining, all his life, a reflexive modesty that made his achievements seem even more admirable. As an actor, he made his name with a decade of great performances, in *Cat on a Hot Tin Roof*, *The Hustler*, *Hud* and *Cool Hand Luke.* He followed up with the popular blockbusters *Butch Cassidy and the Sundance Kid* and *The Sting*, which teamed him forever in the public's mind with his costar and pal Robert Redford. Toward the end of his 60-plus-film career he slipped out of this heartthrob skin to play worn, life-scarred gladiators in *The Color of Money* and *Empire Falls*—the former of which finally brought him, after six nominations, a Best Actor Oscar.

Yet acting was only part of who he was. Newman feared the flatteries of Hollywood and fought hard to lead a rich, full and very private life away from cameras and reporters. He largely succeeded at that as well, enjoying a 50-year marriage to actress Joanne Woodward and raising a family in leafy Westport, Conn. Car racing, which he pursued with passion for nearly 40 years, provided an outlet for a fierce competitive streak and a down-to-earth camaraderie he craved. "Racing," he said, "is the best way I know to get away from all the rubbish of Hollywood." Still, there was more. In 1980, on a lark, Newman decided to bottle some of his homemade salad dressing, sell it and give the money to charity. That whim evolved into the food company Newman's Own, which now markets more than 150 products and gives 100 percent of its profits to charities—$250 million so far. Some of the money goes to the Hole in the Wall Gang camps, a no-cost summer refuge for seriously ill children. Newman, who visited often, was moved by the strength of the kids and the dedication of the counselors. "There," he said, "is where you see what the real grace of this country is, and its power, and its conscience."

Newman died on Sept. 26 after a long and private battle with cancer. The actor-philanthropist "was the last to acknowledge what he was doing was special," his five daughters said in a statement. "Always and to the end, Dad was incredibly grateful for his good fortune. In his own words, 'It's been a pleasure to be here.'" Said Robert Redford: "My life—and this country—is better for his being in it."

A MAN IN FULL Clockwise from top left: in 1969's *Winning*, the film that inspired him to race; with Joanne Woodward (in 1965); with Elizabeth Taylor in *Cat on a Hot Tin Roof*; with Robert Redford in *Butch Cassidy*; in *Cool Hand Luke*; and directing (1984).

CHARLTON
HESTON
1923–2008
APRIL 5

*THE TEN
COMMANDMENTS*
Heston's portrayal of
Moses has become
part of cultural
memory. "He was so
suited to grand roles,"
said onetime costar
Leigh Taylor-Young.

H

HE WAS AMONG THE LAST of his kind: an epic movie star. In a five-decade career, Charlton Heston portrayed the likes of Ben-Hur, Moses and Taylor, the angry hero of *Planet of the Apes*. Offscreen he became almost as well known for his outspoken politics, chiefly as president of the National Rifle Association from 1998 to 2003 (he proclaimed that if gun control advocates wished to take away his firearms, they'd have to pry them "from my cold, dead hands"). Like his friend Ronald Reagan, Heston was a one-time liberal—he'd marched with Rev. Martin Luther King Jr. and backed both John and Robert Kennedy—who later made a sharp right turn. Though he could be a firebrand in public, colleagues remembered "Chuck" as unfailingly gracious. "The sweetest man in the world, kind and thoughtful to all the cast and crew," said actor Robert Vaughn, an extra in 1956's *The Ten Commandments*. Heston, who had been married to his wife, Lydia, for 64 years, died from complications from Alzheimer's but refused to be glum after receiving his diagnosis in 2002. "I got to be Charlton Heston for almost 80 years," he told a friend. "That's more than fair."

AFTER A STINT IN THE AIR FORCE, Roy Scheider—a boxer from Orange, N.J.—scored a big break, and a Best Supporting Actor Oscar nomination, as a cop in 1971's *The French Connection*. But it was his role as the heroic island police chief in *Jaws* (1975) that made him a movie star. "No one anticipated the universal fear of water," said Scheider of the movie's impact. Not to mention the allure of a killer shark. Still, he preferred his work as choreographer Bob Fosse's alter ego in 1979's *All That Jazz*, which scored him another Oscar nod.

ROY SCHEIDER
1932–2008
FEBRUARY 10

SYDNEY POLLACK
1934–2008
MAY 26

AN ACTOR, PRODUCER AND director of 20 films, Sydney Pollack specialized in big movies with big stars, telling *The New York Times* in 1982, "stars are like Thoroughbreds...when they do what they do best—whatever it is that's made them a star—it's really exciting." He made seven films with Robert Redford and won an Oscar for 1985's *Out of Africa*. Tom Cruise recalled Pollack as a man "unpretentious and never condescending," who shared "what he loved about family, storytelling, food, flying and a great bottle of vino." Said Nicole Kidman: "He guided me artistically and personally, not just as a director or producer but as a mentor and a friend."

"Sydney made the world a little better, movies a little better and even dinner a little better," said George Clooney. "A tip of the hat to a class act."

GEORGE
CARLIN
1937–2008
JUNE 22

> " Tonight's forecast:
> Dark. Continued mostly
> dark tonight turning to
> widely scattered light in
> the morning "

WHEN GEORGE CARLIN WAS IN HIS teens, his mother found a list of dirty words in his wallet. Young George explained how he liked writing down colorful curses he'd hear in his New York City neighborhood. That night, "I heard her talking to my uncle," Carlin recalled in a 2004 National Public Radio interview, "saying, 'I think he may need a psychiatrist.'" Instead, he spent more than half a century making people laugh. Before his June 22 death from heart failure at age 71, Carlin recorded more than 20 comedy albums, won four Grammys, taped 14 HBO specials and wrote three bestsellers, mostly based on his vitriolic view of the human race. But his signature moment was "Seven Words You Can Never Say on Television," a routine deemed indecent by the U.S. Supreme Court in 1978. "Before him, comics aspired to put on nice suits and perform in Las Vegas," said Jay Leno. "George rebelled against that life."

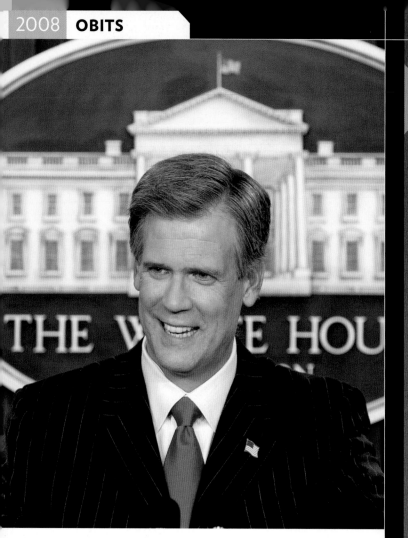

MICHAEL CRICHTON
1942–2008
NOVEMBER 4

CREATIVE WRITING
"Michael was a gentle soul who reserved his flamboyant side for his novels," Spielberg said of his friend, whose successes (above, *ER*) included books, movies and TV.

TONY SNOW
1955–2008
JULY 12

FROM THE PODIUM OF THE WHITE HOUSE briefing room, Tony Snow was every bit the happy warrior, parrying with reporters and defending President Bush's policies with pungent sound bites. Once the cameras were off, however, he liked a good laugh. "People would do a Tony Snow impersonation, and he'd say, 'Do it in front of me,'" recalled Josh Deckard, assistant press secretary during Snow's 17-month tenure. "He didn't take himself too seriously." Added FOX reporter Greta Van Susteren: "He never said a mean word about anybody." In July, Snow lost a three-year battle with colon cancer. An avid musician, he cherished time at home with wife Jill and their three children. "Love," he had said during treatment, citing family and friends, "is a valuable and precious thing."

HE WAS—LITERALLY—A literary giant: a congenial 6'9" former basketball player who towered over his fans at signings. Yet Michael Crichton, who died at age 66 on Nov. 4 after a private battle with throat cancer, will be remembered most for the immensity of his gift. The author of 15 suspense-filled novels (10 became movies), he wrote books like *The Andromeda Strain*, his first bestseller, *Disclosure* and *The Terminal Man*. The creator of NBC's *ER* had "talent [that] outscaled even his own dinosaurs," said Steven Spielberg, who directed Crichton's *Jurassic Park*, which grossed close to $1 billion. "There is no one in the wings that will ever take his place."

SHE MADE A CAREER OUT OF FEISTY. AS Harvey Fierstein's mom in *Torch Song Trilogy*. As Cher's mom in *Mask*. And, most memorably, as Bea Arthur's wisecracking mother, Sophia, in *The Golden Girls*. "I met her and I just said, 'I've got her!'" said *Girls* creator Susan Harris of the day she cast Getty. "She was a New York mother. She had those rhythms. What made her so lovable was she could say anything." Getty, who passed away on July 22 after a long illness, grew up on Manhattan's Lower East Side and began her career performing one-liners in the Catskills. In 1947 she married businessman Arthur Gettleman (whose last name she modified into her stage name), and continued to work in and out of showbiz while raising two sons. "She was a whirlwind as a young mother—working, auditioning, shopping, cleaning," said her son Barry, 55. "And she was a brilliant actress."

ESTELLE GETTY
1923–2008
JULY 22

CAROL BURNETT WANTED HARVEY KORMAN FOR HER NEW TV variety show and wasn't shy about asking him. "I was in the CBS lot and there he was, about to get into his car," she recalled. "I pushed him over the hood and said, 'Please, you've got to do my show.' Obviously, it worked out." Before *The Carol Burnett Show*, which ran from 1967 to 1978, the Chicago-born Korman had made his name doing bit parts. *Burnett*, the perfect showcase for his parodic gifts, made him a star. "His timing was impeccable—he was the best," said Mel Brooks, who cast Korman as the wily politico Hedley ("not Hedy!") Lamarr in the comedy classic *Blazing Saddles*. When *Burnett* ended, Korman, who died of complications from an aneurism, toured with costar Tim Conway. "Whatever I'd say," said Conway, whose ad-libs were a constant threat to equilibrium, "he'd fall down." Wed 25 years to second wife Deborah, Korman had four children. "He was my best friend," said daughter Kate, 25. "He made people feel special, like the only person in the room."

HARVEY KORMAN
1927–2008
MAY 29

COCONSPIRATORS "He was never jealous—he'd be the first to applaud," said Mel Brooks of Korman (with pal and costar Tim Conway).

"GIRL, YOU BETTER COME ABOARD THIS train," Bernie Mac told his future wife, Rhonda, when they began dating in high school, "because I'm gonna be *rich*." The brashly confident comic endured years of struggle—and a job driving a Wonder Bread delivery truck—before victory in a national talent contest led to a spot on HBO's *Def Comedy Jam,* the Original Kings of Comedy tour and movie and, eventually, *The Bernie Mac Show* on Fox. His sudden death, at 50, shocked family and friends. Mac—born Bernard McCullough—had long suffered from sarcoidosis, a chronic condition that can cause inflammation of the lungs. A July trip to the hospital was thought to be almost routine, but Mac quickly succumbed to pneumonia and a second strain of infection. "His presence is there in our home," Rhonda McCullough, 50, his wife of 30 years, said after the funeral. "I get through because I know he's in a better place now."

BERNIE
MAC
1957–2008
AUGUST 9

HE WAS A GENIUS, AND PRACTICAL. "Learning how to think," David Foster Wallace told students at Kenyon College in 2005, "really means learning how to exercise some control over how and what you think . . . being conscious and aware enough to choose what you pay attention to . . . how you construct meaning from experience. Because, if you cannot exercise this kind of choice in life, you will be totally hosed." Wallace became one of the leading literary lights of his generation with the publication, in 1996, of his 1,079-page novel *Infinite Jest*. Few knew he suffered for years from severe depression—a condition he described, in *Jest*, as being "lonely on a level that cannot be conveyed. . . . Everything is part of the problem, and there is no solution. It is hell for one." Even electroconvulsive therapy brought no relief. On Sept. 12 he hanged himself. Said his father, James: "He just couldn't stand it anymore."

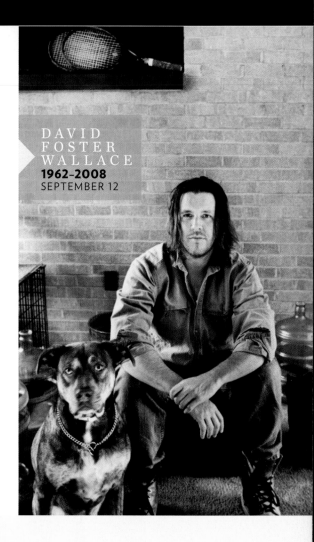

DAVID
FOSTER
WALLACE
1962–2008
SEPTEMBER 12

CHRISTOPHER
BOWMAN
1967–2008
JANUARY 10

IN THE EARLY '90s HE'D BEEN "BOWMAN the Showman," the two-time U.S. men's skating champion who wowed fans with speed and showmanship. By March of 2007 he had ballooned to over 250 lbs. and was giving lessons in rented skates. "He said his own had been stolen," recalled a fellow instructor.

It had been a long, well-documented trip down. After representing the U.S. at the 1992 Olympics, where he finished fourth, Bowman struggled with drugs, alcohol, rehab and a painful divorce. On Jan. 10, 2008, he was found dead in the Budget Inn in North Hills, Calif. "He had been drinking heavily," said the county coroner. "He had taken Vicodin the night before and had a history of cocaine abuse."

"Chris had a bad-boy quality," said skater Scott Hamilton. But "he never uttered a bad word about anyone." Said Chris's mom, Joyce Bowman: "He thought he was put on this earth to have a good time."

THE FAMILY HAD BEEN ON VACATION IN Rome, but NBC newsman Tim Russert had to leave early to return to Washington to host *Meet the Press*. He hated saying goodbye; so did his wife, journalist Maureen Orth. "I said, 'I want to give you a hug. I don't know if I'll ever see you again,'" she recalled later. "I don't know why I said that to him. I just had a feeling."

Tragically, she was right to worry. The next day, Russert, 58, collapsed at work and died of a heart attack. The shock and sadness among friends and colleagues—and thousands of fans of *Big Russ and Me*, his moving account of his Depression-era father raising a baby-boomer son—was palpable. "Family and faith were the foundations of his life," wrote his friend Tom Brokaw, who called Russert "America's premier political journalist." Said Orth: "I had no idea Tim meant so much to so many." She took some solace from the joy her husband had found and readily shared. "Tim was a happy man," she said. "He realized all of his dreams."

TIM
RUSSERT
1950–2008
JUNE 13

ISAAC HAYES
1942–2008
AUGUST 10

AS A PRODUCER, ISAAC Hayes helped shape the sound of the Stax Records soul factory in its '70s prime; as a singer, he wrote and recorded the classic "Theme from *Shaft*," which brought him, in 1972, the first Best Original Song Oscar ever awarded to an African-American. As an actor, he appeared on TV and in movies and, from 1997 to 2006, dished out salty wisdom as the animated cafeteria worker Chef on *South Park*. Through it all—acting, performing or just being—Hayes, who died at 65 of a stroke, radiated cool. Contemporary musicians tried to capture it by sampling his songs. When young record execs asked what he was up to, Hayes once said, he'd think to himself, "Just turn on the radio and listen to some of your hip-hop stuff. *That's* what I've done lately."

RANDY PAUSCH
1960–2008
JULY 25

A STAR IN HIS ACADEMIC FIELD, Carnegie Mellon computer science professor Randy Pausch, 47, catapulted to fame after he delivered the university's traditional Last Lecture in September 2007. Intended to showcase a professor's personal philosophy, the lecture in Pausch's case really would be one of his last: Diagnosed with pancreatic cancer, he'd recently been told he had, at best, six months to live. Filled with the kind of simple yet sage advice Pausch had always given his students—never give up on your dreams; find the best in others; have fun—the lecture went viral on the Internet, drawing 10 million new listeners. *The Last Lecture*, a follow-up book that expanded on his thoughts, became a global phenomenon and is now published in 30 languages. Pausch, married and a father of three young children, died July 25. "Randy," said his sister Tamara Mason, "had magic."

"He's a complicated man, but no one understands him but his woman . . . John Shaft!"
—A LYRIC FROM HAYES' GREATEST HIT, 'SHAFT'

CHAIN MALE
At his peak, Hayes (in L.A. in 1972) stood atop the Everest of outlandish macho-soul.

RAISED IN KNOXVILLE, TENN., BRAD Renfro was just 10 when he was picked to play a gutsy witness in a Mafia case in 1994's *The Client*; the next year he won *The Hollywood Reporter*'s "Young Star Award." In the months before his death, Renfro—who made more than 20 movies, including *Ghost World* and *Deuces Wild*—had just wrapped a part alongside Billy Bob Thornton in *The Informers* and "had been working hard and was very focused on the future," said his attorney Richard Kaplan. The years in between, though, included a sad history of drug abuse and a string of drug-related run-ins with the law. Autopsy results showed Renfro died from an accidental heroin overdose. The first time he was busted—at age 15, for possessing cocaine and marijuana—he said he had learned a lesson about taking drugs. "If you've never done it, don't," the actor, who struck many as a special talent, told PEOPLE after his 1998 arrest. "If you have done it, pray."

BRAD
RENFRO
1982-2008
JANUARY 15

BOBBY
FISCHER
1943-2008
JANUARY 17

AT THE CHESS BOARD, HE VANquished opponents with breathtaking genius. In life, though, Bobby Fischer seemed to fall victim to a more formidable foe—his own inner demons. Raised in Brooklyn, he began playing chess at age 6. By 15, he had become the youngest grand master in the game's history. In 1972, in the depths of the Cold War, he traveled to Reykjavik, Iceland, to play Boris Spassky of the Soviet Union for the world championship. Fischer won, becoming the first American-born chess champion, as well as a national hero. But Fischer wound up retreating into his own world, dropping out of sight for 20 years, then becoming known for his anti-Semitic and anti-American rants. Still, says his biographer Frank Brady, "his games will live forever."

HIS LIST OF FASHION INNO- vations includes the trapeze dress, women's tuxedo suits and safari chic, yet there was at least one style staple Yves Saint Laurent regretted not being able to take credit for. "Years ago he said, 'I wish I had invented blue jeans,'" recalled one of his former models, Iman. "He always had it in the back of his mind to design for the modern woman." Even without denim, that's what Saint Laurent—who died in his Paris apartment of a brain tumor—did, whether putting women in Russian-inspired peasant looks or art-print dresses. Says embroiderer Jean-Francois Lesage: "He reinvented everything."

YVES
SAINT
LAURENT
1936–2008
JUNE 01

SUZANNE PLESHETTE
1937–2008
JANUARY 19

UNDERCOVER Pleshette with Bob Newhart on *The Bob Newhart Show*.

A MOVIE AND TV VETERAN, SUZANNE PLESHETTE was looking forward to receiving a star on Hollywood's Walk of Fame, scheduled for Jan. 31, 2008. It was about time, she noted in an invitation to friends, adding that she was delighted the star would appear just outside of Frederick's of Hollywood: "Where else?"

Sadly, she missed her big day. Pleshette—a longtime smoker who had been diagnosed with lung cancer in 2006—died of respiratory failure in her L.A. home on Jan. 19. "She fought tooth and nail," said her friend Nikki Haskell. "She was in so much pain. The war is over."

Most famous for playing Bob Newhart's sassy schoolteacher wife on *The Bob Newhart Show* in the '70s, Pleshette was known among friends for her loyalty and salty language. "She could swear like a sailor, yet she was very loving and caring," said Haskell. She wed her third husband, actor Tom Poston (who occasionally appeared on *Bob Newhart* and co-starred on the subsequent *Newhart*), in 2001; he died in 2007. Her friends will remember her as the life of any and every party. "When you saw Suzanne leave," said author Jackie Collins, "it was time to go."